Fresh Bread

30 Day Devotional for Purpose Filled Living

By Julia A. Royston

Edited by: Claude R. Royston

BK Royston Publishing, LLC
Jeffersonville, IN

BK Royston Publishing
P. O. Box 4321
Jeffersonville, IN 47131
502-802-5385
http://bkroystonpublishing.com
bkroystonpublishing@gmail.com

© Copyright – 2015

All Rights Reserved. No part of this book may be reproduced, stored in a retrieval system, or transmitted by any means without the written permission of the author.

Published by: BK Royston Publishing LLC
Cover photo licensed by: Shutterstock.com
Layout: BK Royston Publishing LLC

ISBN-13: 978-0692501405

ISBN-10: 0692501401

LCCN: 2015912334

Printed in the United States of America

Dedication

I dedicate this book to every person who feels that they are currently in a stale, old or stagnant situation or position.

Let one or more than one of these devotionals provide the sustenance, strength and courage that you need to move forward and live that abundant life.

In 30 days, you can change a habit which can change a position which can change your life.

Acknowledgement

I thank my Lord and Savior Jesus Christ for giving me another opportunity to introduce more people to you. I thank you that you have entrusted this gift to me. Lord, let your Spirit move, guide and empower through this book to the people who will read it.

To my husband, Brian K. Royston, the love of my life for loving and cheering me on so much that I can be and do all that God has placed in me. I love you...

To my Mom, my greatest supporter and best friend. To my Dad, who is in heaven, that I know is proud of me and always encouraged me to go for it. Thanks to all of the rest of my family for their love and support.

A special thank you to Rev. and Mrs. Claude R. Royston for their love and support. Papa thank you for using your fine tooth comb to edit yet another book for me.

Love, Julia A. Royston

Introduction

I love fresh bread. There is nothing like hot croissants, yeast roll or biscuit with butter dripping on top and some great preserves mix on top of that. When the bread is placed in your mouth, there is something powerful and euphoric that moves from your mouth to your toes. Fresh hot and good bread is heavenly.

The Lord's Prayer says, "Give us our daily bread," Matthew 6:19 Bread is a natural food group. It provides a portion of necessary nutrients to sustain life. Jesus said, "I am the bread of life," John 6:41. In John 6:51 Jesus said, "I am the living bread.." Jesus is that bread for everlasting life. God's word to a follower is that spiritual nutrient that will not only sustain life but, expand your life.

Prepare yourself for 30 days of His freshest bread. God bless you…

Table of Contents

A Creature for the Creator and Not Just Creatures of Habit	1
A Gift to You, Give it Back to the World and it is Passed on…	5
An Ample Supply	9
Calm Down and Rest in the Lord	13
Christian Witness Credentials	17
Don't Get Out of Line	21
Faith	Obey	Follow - "Bet on Jesus"	25
For This Cause…	29
Fresh Bread	33
From A Risk To Reward	37
God's Favorite	43
He knows the Way, the What and the Who	47
Help for the Harvest	51
I'm Not Little	55
Inhabit, Inclination and Inherited	59

Just Believe Because Fat Meat is Still Greasy and God can make the Impossible Easy	63
Love it and Show it	67
Make The Adjustment	71
Partners for a Purpose	75
Power Down to Power Up	79
Repair, Remove, Replace	83
Season of Need	87
Smell of Victory	91
Standing Alone	95
The God Effect	99
The Grace with My Gift	103
The Trust Factor	107
The Power of One	111
What do you see?	115

Who changed the truth of God into a lie, and worshipped and served the creature more than the Creator, who is blessed forever. Amen. Romans 1:25 (KJV)

A Creature for the Creator and Not Just Creatures of Habit

I recently had an epiphany of sorts. I was teaching a kindergarten class and it was time for them to leave. The bell had rung so we were late. Instead of the students being instructed to go to the carpet, sit down and wait for their homeroom teacher, like normal, I told them to push in their chairs, get their personal belongings and line up in order at the door. Because of the routine established since August, all of the students went to the carpet and sat down. Not one student lined up at the door. They followed the normal routine and stuck to it no matter what I said. These little people are clearly "creatures of habit." I was amazed. I was stunned. Not one child, the informer or 'the know it all,' said, "Mrs. Royston told us to go line up at the door," as I would have expected. Each child followed the routine instead of my instructions. I was taught by veteran teachers that children are creatures of habit and to control them, maintain order and have a productive class, they must do the same thing over and over again. You must repeat the same instructions over and over again. If you divert from the routine, all will be lost. As a public school teacher and educator, I would have been applauded for instilling routines in my students and maintaining behavior management.

On the other hand, God taught me a lesson. What if He gave you an instruction different from your normal routine? Will you follow it? Will you ignore what I said and prefer what has happened in the past or your normal routine? All habits are not bad. All routine is not bad. But, what is bad is if you miss an opportunity, blessing, message, answer or divine appointment necessary for your next destination because you were stuck in your routine. I agree, God will always get you where He wants you. But, in the bible are many examples of the part that each of us must play in the miracle. He taught me that my top priority is to be a creature to be used and directed by the creator and not a creature of habit who relies on the routine as the only route for God to release your blessing. God bless you.

Prayer: Lord, I thank you that you are the creator of mankind. Let me be a creature who awaits instructions from you. You are the creator. In Jesus' name I pray. Amen!

But not as the offence, so also is the free gift. For if through the offence of one many be dead, much more the grace of God, and the gift by grace, which is by one man, Jesus Christ, hath abounded unto many.   Romans 5:15 (KJV)

A Gift to You, Give it Back to the World and it is Passed on...

During Christmas, we all love gifts. I love to give them and enjoy receiving gifts as well. The ultimate gift in any season is the gift of redemption and salvation from God through Jesus Christ. When we accept him, we accept his very costly free gift. The gift cost Jesus His life and a horrible death on the cross.

Besides the gift of salvation, we are given some other inner gifts, talents and natural abilities. God has given to us even more gifts through Jesus Christ. It is amazing how many more gifts are revealed when our lives are turned over to Him. Our job is to discover, develop and distribute our gifts to the world. These gifts are to the glory and honor of God, not ourselves. Oh what a responsibility, oh what a privilege it is to be given such a gift. So it is a cycle, system and circle of life. God gives us gifts and then we perfect the gift to give out to others. God continues to restore, empower, anoint and assign our gifts. We are to use these gifts to benefit others. He then continues to bless, prosper and promote us as we use our gifts for His glory and to build His children and Kingdom! He is a giver who keeps on giving, gifts that keep on multiplying to people who will keep on receiving.

Prayer: Thank you Father for the many gifts you have down inside of me. Let me use each one to your glory and your honor. Have your way in my life. In Jesus' name I pray. Amen.

But my God shall supply all your need according to his riches in glory by Christ Jesus. Philippians 4:19 (KJV)

An Ample Supply

My father ran a successful janitorial service for more than forty years. He believed in having supplies for his employees. He had cabinets built in our home garage, storage in the back yard, off-site storage and a warehouse for supplies. My dad always had an ample supply of equipment to get the job done even when he had 50 plus employees. My father passed away in May 2010. When we were cleaning out the house, I found a huge box of small bags that we used to put in the small trash cans in each office. More than four years later, I am still using those bags. I laughed one day when I thought about my dad having such a great amount of supplies that he was still supplying me with janitorial supplies even after his death. Well, if my earthly, biological father provided that much supply, what about our heavenly Father? All of the earth, heaven and the universe is His. All of the silver, gold, power, glory and authority belongs to Him. He is the ultimate creator so if it doesn't exist, He can give somebody the idea to create it or just speak His word and it will come into existence. So in Philippians 4:19 Paul said, "God shall supply all your need according to His riches in glory by Christ Jesus." What do you stand in need of today? God has an ample, over abundant store house to supply that need today. Ask Him. Wait for Him. Prepare to receive from Him. For my God shall supply it.

Prayer: Father I thank you that you are my Jehovah Jireh, my provider. You never run out and never decrease. I praise you for a never ending ample supply. In Jesus' name. Amen.

Be anxious for nothing, but in everything by prayer and supplication, with thanksgiving, let your requests be made known to God. Philippians 4:6

And the peace of God, which passeth all understanding, shall keep your hearts and minds through Christ Jesus. Philippians 4:7

Rest in the Lord, and wait patiently for Him; Do not fret because of him who prospers in his way, Because of the man who brings wicked schemes to pass. Psalm 27:7 (NKJV)

Calm Down and Rest in the Lord

As a teacher, I have had students come running up to me upset or even happy about what someone said or did to them in class or even something great that happened to them. At times, they have been running, crying and so hyper that their breathing was choppy from being out of breath. I have been nervous that a student was about to have an asthma or panic attack right in front of me because the situation made them so excited, upset and/or angry. They can't tell me and I won't understand what they are even saying until they calm down. Are you so anxious or complaining about the problem that you can't hear God's answer? God is waiting on you to calm down, come to Him, collect the instructions and then complete the assignment. The solution to the issue may be right in front of you but, you are so upset, frantic and focused on the problem that you miss the answer. There was a child who came to me upset about missing her headband but, another child had already given the head band to me earlier that day. She is standing there fussing about the head band and I had it. I said, stop fussing, get your head band and go back to class. To some of you God is saying, calm down and listen to me because I have the answer. Receive your answer and go on to victory. You can't hear while you are complaining. Calm down, listen and the answer will come.

Prayer: Father I know you are concerned about every area of my life. Help me to calm down, turn it over to you and wait for the answer. In Jesus' name. Amen.

Ye are my witnesses, saith the Lord, and my servant whom I have chosen: Isaiah 43:10 (KJV)

Christian Witness Credentials

I am a sports fan and my favorite sport is football. I watch ESPN all of the time and admire all of the commentators who speak about the various sports, the players, owners, coaches and the game itself. I love it because when each commentator is speaking, his resume summary or brief credentials of their accomplishments appears right under their image on the screen. The credentials can read MVP of the Super Bowl, 3-time Pro Bowl attendee, Writer for one of the Sports columns, Coach of the year or even Front Office member of the year. There are some reasons why they are making a comment on that sport, player or issue. They have sports credentials. Have you ever wondered why you are going through what's going on in your life? You are getting your Christian Witness Credentials. God needs a witness and He is going to use you. After Lazarus was raised from the dead after a long illness, four days in the grave and the beginning stages of decomposition of his body, Jesus used Lazarus' newly acquired Christian Witness Credentials to continue to confirm that He was truly the Son of God. We now know that Jesus is the Son of God through all of the miracles in the bible but, people in the earth still need to know that God is real even today.

So, when you survive a trial or a tribulation pull out your Christian Witness Credentials which tell others that God has used His power inside of you. "Ye are of God, little children, and have overcome them: because greater is he that is in you, than he that is in the world." I John 4:4 (KJV)

Next, when you go through a storm and remain a worshipper the enemy realizes that your relationship with God is real. "Many are the afflictions of the righteous: but the Lord delivereth him out of them all." Psalms 34: 19 (KJV)

"Fear ye not, neither be afraid: have not I told thee from that time, and have declared it? ye are even my witnesses. Is there a God beside me? yea, there is no God; I know not any." Isaiah 44:8 (KJV)

Finally, God needs earthly witnesses for others to keep going, persevere and know that He is real and can use anybody and certainly YOU! You all are hereby, certifiably confirmed to have received, renewed and are everlasting members of the Kingdom of God with your Christian Witness Credentials.

Prayer: Father I thank you that you are omnipotent. All power is in your hands. Help me to stand strong and be your witness in the earth. In Jesus' name. Amen.

Wherefore take unto you the whole armour of God, that ye may be able to withstand in the evil day, and having done all, to stand. Ephesians 6:13

Don't Get Out of Line

During the 2012 U. S. Presidential election, we waited until the wee hours of the morning to see if President Barack Obama would be re-elected. A lot had been said and done on the campaign trail but, it was still that November night that would decide who would be the President of the United States for the next four years. I am an avid social media person. Okay, I confess, I am a social media addict. I watched social media closely rather than the television as people sent messages to people in Ohio and Florida to not get out of line but, keep waiting to vote because their vote was so critical to the President's re-election. People posted, "hold somebody else's spot", "we're counting on you Ohio and Florida" or "You can do it, etc." Needless to say, the necessary votes were cast and President Obama was re-elected to serve four more years.

There are things in your life that are going to require that you hold your position, take your stance and not back down. Don't get out of line when it comes to your family, your health, desires, dreams and destiny. Pastor Shirley Caesar recorded a famous song, "You're next in line for a miracle." If you get out of line, you won't be next in line. When you move out of position, you give the power to someone else. Just like those people who were determined to stand in line to cast their vote for a man they believe in, whom they may never meet, you must be willing to stand your ground for what you believe. Hold to your beliefs and watch God bring it to pass. Above all, don't get out of line.

Prayer: Lord, I thank you that you had power to take a stand against the powers on this earth. Give me the courage and power to stand up for what I believe in for you. In Jesus' Name I pray. Amen.

Now when Jesus heard these things, he said unto him, Yet lackest thou one thing: sell all that thou hast, and distribute unto the poor, and thou shalt have treasure in heaven: and come, follow me. Luke 18:22 (KJV)

Faith | Obey | Follow
"Bet on Jesus"

First, this devotion is not an advocate for gambling in any way. From my youth, I was taught not to bet or gamble but, this is the title God gave me. I have been in prayer about direction for my businesses and ministry. God brought this scripture to me. Luke 18:22 is the story of the rich young ruler. The rich young ruler came to Jesus asking how he could inherit eternal life. Jesus said, keep the commandments. The young ruler said, I have done that from my youth. He meant by that "I do that already and that is not hard." Next Jesus went for the jugular and addressed the rich young ruler's money. Jesus told somebody rich to sell everything, give it away and follow me. The rich young ruler went away sorrowful and disappointed by Jesus' request. He wasn't willing to do it. He wasn't willing to risk everything and bet on Jesus. The rich young ruler had faith in Jesus because he came and asked him the question. He felt he obeyed the commandments because he kept them from his youth but, that request right before the "follow me" was a bit much.

Has God ever asked you to give up something that you really loved simply because he said it? There was no promise of a blessing, super breakthrough or answer to a prayer. God just wants you to trust him, obey what he has commanded and continue to follow Him.

The money is not the moral of the story. The story is an unwillingness to give up your treasure for God's eternal treasure. The moral is "Bet on Jesus". Risk it all for Him. Risk your time, talents and treasure for Him. Give up your way of thinking, ideas and take on God's. Believe him. Obey Him. Follow Him. There is no telling where you will go and what he will do through you. Bet on Jesus.

Prayer: Father I thank you that you love me and want what's best for me. Help me to trust, obey and follow you on your command. In Jesus' name I pray. Amen.

Pilate therefore said unto him, Art thou a king then? Jesus answered, Thou sayest that I am a king. To this end was I born, and for this cause came I into the world, that I should bear witness unto the truth. Every one that is of the truth heareth my voice. John 18:37

For This Cause…

When Jesus spoke these words to Pilate, He stood on the brink of a crucial destiny moment. The culmination of Jesus' existence and the reason for His birth was in this statement. Jesus had done so many wonderful things in His short time on earth that they couldn't all be recorded. Despite His wonderful works to all men, Calvary was the reason for His birth. Redemption, reconciliation and salvation for all mankind would be bought and paid for after the death of Jesus. Is there a "for this cause" in your life? What are you doing that you know that God called you, appointed you and your anointing flows freely completing that assignment? I had a "for this cause" experience with God. One day, I was driving and praying about my purpose. God spoke to me specifically about my "for this cause" assignment. The very thing that He said was the reason for my birth to do on earth is the least desirable and takes a lot out of me physically, emotionally and intellectually. I have noticed that when I fulfill my assignment, I feel the most inadequate but, when I need God the most. Jesus' death on the cross was the most horrific experience ever but, the requirement of God for Him was the price for eternal life for mankind. It took all of heaven and earth in Him to fulfill that assignment but, He did it. We will thank Him forever for making that sacrifice. In the end, what is your "for this cause" assignment? The world is waiting…

Prayer: Father, I thank you that you loved me enough to die for me. That was your assignment. Help me to realize and fulfill my assignment for your glory. In Jesus' name I pray. Amen.

And the children of Israel did eat manna forty years, until they came to a land inhabited; they did eat manna, until they came unto the borders of the land of Canaan.
Exodus 16:35 (KJV)

Fresh Bread

One of my family's favorite food to eat at dinner was bread. My father gained the most weight when my mother started making homemade rolls. He gained so much weight that he told my mother to stop making them. We all laughed but, we loved bread. My middle sister would come home from school and just toast bread, butter it and eat it plain without jelly because she loved bread so much. There is nothing like fresh hot bread, right out of the oven. The butter takes only seconds to melt and it seems like it takes fewer seconds to eat. My husband even loves bread more than I do. He likes bread at every meal. We have no children but, we still have to buy multiple loaves of bread when shopping at the grocery store. My biological family was only five people. My parents, myself and two sisters. My family now is just me and my husband. But, imagine providing fresh bread for thousands of families and it is estimated between 4 and 6 million people every single day. (http://lavistachurchofchrist.org/LVanswers/2004/2004-07-10a.htm).

God did that each and every day. When the children of Israel came out of Egypt, they were headed to Canaan, the promise land. After fear came and they followed the advice of ten out of twelve spies, they landed in the wilderness for 40 years eating manna every day provided by heaven's bakery. Manna was truly fresh bread delivered at their door step each and every day. God's word is Fresh bread to you every day from God. Enjoy!

Prayer: Father I thank you that you truly are a provider. All that I need you have provided for me my whole life. Help me to open my eyes to the fresh bread that you have for me each day. In Jesus' name I pray. Amen.

And let us not be weary in well doing: for in due season we shall reap, if we faint not. Galatians 6:9 (KJV)

From A Risk To Reward

I spent 10 years being the librarian and computer teacher at a private all girls' high school. I was recruited first, because they needed a librarian and I had a degree in librarianship. Secondly, I was recruited because they had no African American persons on staff. Not one. They told me that they loved and enjoyed having me but, couldn't believe that I stayed the ten years before going on to public school. The only Black people who stayed longer than me had been the culinary and custodian staff.

The goal of the school in 1996, was to recruit and offer scholarships to African American girls specifically. They wanted to increase diversity in their enrollment. They felt with a minority staff member it could help with retention, matriculation and hopefully, graduation. The girls they recruited were skilled and academically astute but, economically ineligible and potentially, "at risk."

I have been in public elementary school now for 9 years. The first two years as the librarian and since then the computer teacher. I walked into an after school professional development workshop with a young lady who looked very familiar. We walked in together and I asked her if her name was, "Lynn" and she said, "no." But, we kept walking together because we were headed to the same room. I never forget a face but, I am terrible with names.

I sat behind her in the workshop because her fellow teachers from her school wanted to sit together. It bothered me so much that I said during a break, "make me know you. Where do you go to church? I know I know you. Why do I know you?" She said, "You are Ms. Foree." When she said that, I knew that she was one of my former students from the private school. I was only Ms. Foree in public school for two months prior to getting married. This young woman was now a teacher. She had been one of my students. She was vocal when she needed to be but, highly intelligent, organized, took advantage of every opportunity at school and was determined to be something one day. I asked her what was her major in college and she said, "Biology." Wow, I flunked Biology in the eleventh grade and had to go to summer school so that floored me. She said, "I just graduated and got my master's degree in teaching last spring and this is my first year teaching." I asked her was she single or married. She said, "I am waiting on him to find me." I nearly cried. This was one of my "at risk" students. Given a chance, she took full advantage of the opportunity and made it. The school had taken a chance on me, they took a chance on her and we all reaped the benefits and were rewarded for the chance accepted and maximized.

What are you willing to take a risk on? It has been 13 years since she graduated high school but, I am now seeing the harvest of my sowing into someone else's life. I love immediate gratification but, the gratification of seeing that young woman with a career, a beautiful car, single, waiting on a husband with no kids, was worth it.

You shall reap if you faint not. Take a risk, give it your best and reap a harvest.

Prayer: Father, I thank you that you have all power. Let me continue and not get tired or stop doing what you called me to do. In Jesus' Name. Amen.

I will look on you with favor and make you fruitful and increase your numbers, and I will keep my covenant with you. Leviticus 26:9

God's Favorite

No matter how hard we try not to have favorite people in our lives, we do. There are people in my life that are my favorite. I admit it. There are certain people that I just enjoy being around. I can be myself with them. I make a connection and I am on the same page with them spiritually and mentally. I don't have to explain myself. I don't have to be cautious about what I say or how I will be interpreted because I feel like they love me for me. Now do I love other people less? No. Do hate other people? No. Am I hesitant to be around certain people by the way they act? Yes. Again, I admit it, I have favorites. God on the other hand, died for us all. God loves us all just the way we are and unconditionally as we are. But, even God says, I will look on you with favor. How is that possible for an all loving God to have favorites? In Leviticus 26, God promised the children of

Israel that He would show His favor upon them if they obeyed Him and kept His Covenant. There is a long list of things that God promised Israel if they would obey Him. Natural parents know that their children have certain rights and favors with you if they obey you. That is no different than the favor that God shows His children. The bible says, that it rains on the just and unjust but, 'Noah found favor in the eyes of the Lord' and it saved his whole family. Moses found favor with God and he was chosen the deliverer of the nation of Israel. Some children don't get what the other children get because they are unwilling to do what the other children do for God. What are you willing to do to receive God's favor? What are you willing to sacrifice, surrender and sanctify yourself from to receive God's favor? Remember God's favor is worth more than money. Because God's favor can get you into some places that money can't buy you. Love God. Obey His Commandments. Be ready to walk in the Favor of God.

Prayer: Father we thank you for your favor on our lives. We have done nothing to earn or deserve your favor. Our desire is to please you in all that we do and say. In Jesus' Name we pray. Amen.

But He knows the way that I take [He has concern for it, appreciates, and pays attention to it]. When He has tried me, I shall come forth as refined gold [pure and luminous].
Job 23:10

He knows the Way, the What and the Who

I am so thankful today for the GPS system because I do not like getting lost. I get panicky and fearful if I don't easily arrive at the location. My husband and I had reservations to take a very leisurely cruise on one of the dinner cruises in Chicago at the Pier. Our GPS system wasn't working correctly on our very old phone. I panicked and started yelling for him to drive toward the water, Lake Michigan. Wow, that was a scene, anything but, relaxing. Have you ever thought, I must be lost, this doesn't look, feel or resemble anything like I believed God for? This is not the bank account, house, car, job, position at church, relationship or child I saw. I shouldn't be here with this, I am lost. I should be_____and you fill in the blank. But, my first pastor used to quote the scripture all of the time, He knows the way that I take. That is from Job 23:10. I can imagine that Job probably thought he was lost after he lost everything, his wife, children and possessions. In spite of the advice and speculations of why everything happened to him from his friends, he realized, ultimately, God knows. He knows the way that I am taking, should take and will take. He knows the what, of what is going on in my life. Nothing has gotten past God. He sees and knows everything from the beginning to the end. Furthermore, He knows who. He knows who I am, where I am and whose I am. I am His and He is mine. He sits high and looks low but, He is so close, He has numbered every hair on my head, even the gray ones. So today no matter what is going on in your life, keep walking, don't stop, keep trusting and keep believing because He knows the way, the what and the who.

Prayer: Father I thank you that you know the way, you have the plan and all power. Help me to follow you. In Jesus' Name. Amen.

And they beckoned unto their partners, which were in the other ship, that they should come and help them. And they came, and filled both the ships, so that they began to sink.
Luke 5:7 (KJV)

Help for the Harvest

Isn't it amazing that with all of the work that you put into a project, product or production, when it is time to harvest or reap what you have sown, you don't have the help to harvest? Friends walk away. Family has long gotten tired of you. You have been saying that you were on the brink of a turn around, walking into your destiny and moving to the next level but, it has taken longer than expected. Now, the harvest is here, the blessing has come but, where is the help that you need to bring it in? What do you do? First, you pray. Then, second, you pray some more. Third, know that God knew that the year, month, day and second that you would need the help to harvest. Finally, know that God has a plan, purpose, provision and persons to help you harvest it. Those people who left, were supposed to leave. Those people who got tired, were supposed to get tired. Those people who didn't believe, God knew they wouldn't believe. "Without faith it is impossible to please God."

So now, look for your help. Your help cometh from the Lord but, He is going to use natural hands, feet and know how to get the job done. It's not too late. You didn't miss it. Nothing is going to spoil in the field. You will bring it. You will reap the harvest. You will succeed. Because God has the help for the harvest.

Prayer: Father we thank you for the help for the harvest. You cannot lie and you made us a promise. We trust and believe you always. In Jesus' Name we pray. Amen.

Samuel said, "Although you were once small in your own eyes, did you not become the head of the tribes of Israel? The Lord anointed you king over Israel.
1 Samuel 15:17

I can do all things through Christ that strengthens me.
Philippians 4:13

Take counsel together, and it shall come to nought; speak the word, and it shall not stand: for God is with us Isaiah 8:10

I'm Not Little

There was an instructional assistant in our building leading a group of children from the computer lab to their individual classrooms. The older students walked down the hall under the watchful eye of the teacher but, the young students were led downstairs to their classroom on the first floor. Prior to leading the younger students, the teacher said, "Alright little ones, let's get in a line and head downstairs." The teacher was leading the line and I was standing at the end of the line still in the computer lab and heard one of the younger students say, "I'm not little." Another child said, "I'm not little either." The younger ones were smaller than the older kids but, the younger child refused to agree with being called little. The Lord asked me when the child spoke those words, "how do you see yourself?" He also reminded me of the scripture in I Samuel 15 and how Saul saw himself as 'small in his own eyes.' Samuel told Saul that you may see yourself as small but, God still anointed you King over all of Israel. You are not small to God but, it is you who thinks you are small, insignificant and not much compared to others. There are times that I get ideas for devotionals from God and forget them but, this one, God would not let me forget until I wrote it. I confess that there are times that I don't see myself as God sees me. I make the unwise gesture of looking at someone else's progress and wonder what is wrong with me. But, when I go back to looking at all God has placed in my hands, I throw up both my hands and tell God, 'thank you.' How do you see yourself? Do you see yourself as small or see yourself as God sees you? God sees you as royalty, priests, princes and princesses. God sees you as a holy nation, armed and dangerous. God sees you powerful, purpose-filled and purpose-driven. God sees you as His Child with all rights and privileges that are due you. How do you see yourself? I'm not little.

Prayer: Lord, you are almighty. Help us not to see ourselves as little compared to the enemy but, we are mighty through God. Father you fight for us and we shall be triumphant. In Jesus' name. Amen.

The thief cometh not, but for to steal, and to kill, and to destroy: I am come that they might have life, and that they might have it more abundantly. John 10:10

Inhabit, Inclination and Inherited

In recent years, I have had multiple surgeries to take care of one issue or another. One surgery was because tumors decided to inhabit my body. I did nothing to bring them on, it just happened. Another surgery was from an inclination. Too much fried food and my gall bladder wouldn't function properly. My own inclination, bad habit caused a health issue that had to be taken care of. Another surgery was a result of and directly related to my heritage. It was passed down from my grandmother Henrietta Foree to my father, Jack C. Foree and now to me Julia Ann K. Foree Royston and one of my sisters Stacey Foree Porter.

God says just like your body, in your life, there are things that inhabit your life on their own accord or set up residence. Like the children of Israel had to remove the inhabitants in the promise land, get rid of anything that is hindering you.

In your life, there will be people to whom you are drawn or inclined to hang out with that may not be good for you. These people are subject to distract you from your true purpose and destiny. Get rid of them.

In your life, there may also be some birth defects or diseases that you inherited just because you were born. Nothing that your grandparents or parents did but, through the bloodline was passed down from generation to generation. If these things are detrimental to your life, you have to get rid of them as well.

Remove anything that you don't need to live the abundant life that God promised whether by inhabitation, inclination or inheritance.

Prayer: Father I thank you that you came and promised me abundant life. Help me to remove from my life anything that wants to hinder, distract or stop me from living that abundant life. In Jesus' name. Amen.

For with God nothing shall be impossible. John 1:37

Just Believe Because Fat Meat is Still Greasy and God can make the Impossible Easy

My grandfather and my father had a saying that "you don't believe fat meat is greasy." Of course, the fat meat usually was referring to some part of the pig whether used for bacon or lard. It was super greasy. I digress. But, the saying was tied to your faith and belief system. The saying was usually used because someone didn't act like they really believed what was being said was actually going to happen. The saying was used with several connotations. Sometimes it was right before a reprimand of a child. Sometimes it has been used before sound advice was given for a friend. At even other times, this saying has been even used in spiritual exhortation that could save or bless someone's life. The saying is a call to put your faith into action so you can heed the warning and avoid the punishment if you were being disciplined or get everything in order because you were about to receive a major blessing. I even use it in my classroom when a student doesn't believe that the program is going to work or if their behavior needs a little modification.

My clarion call to you this morning is just like you know that Lard is 100% greasy know that God is 1000% powerful and able to do what you need Him to do. Just like you know that thick bacon is going to produce twice as much grease, know that God is going to do exceedingly, abundantly above all that you can ask or think according to the power that is working in you. Fat meat is now and will always be greasy but, GOD will be all powerful, all knowing, in total control, King of Kings and Lord of Lords long after the pig is extinct and the enemy is in hell forever.

So no matter what you are going through today remember, Believe and know that there is grease in fat meat but, believing in God will bring you victory and no defeat.

Prayer: Father we thank you that we KNOW that you can do anything. It is in your hands and in your plan. In Jesus' name we pray. Amen.

And now these three remain: faith, hope and love. But the greatest of these is love. I Corinthians 13:13

Love it and Show it

Have you ever seen someone singing a song that really loved to sing? When they are singing, there is a slight or big smile on their face. The days of looking evil, angry or mean while you sing is not attractive. I love to see a singer that really loves to sing. Now, it is even better when they sound good as well as happy singing. I digress. My point is that you should love it. Even more than loving what you do, you should have a love or general interest in the people who see or hear your performance. It will make a difference in how people respond to your performance. Because I am an artist, I watch other artists. I notice that those artists that show interest in their fans or supporters, go further and last longer. Those that do not take an interest in their fans, you can tell the difference. Do others see the love coming through for what you do? The old saying goes that talk is cheap but, actions speak louder than words. If you love it, show it. If you love and show it, others will feel it and then be attracted to it. Love is a verb or an action word. A true love for something or someone will move you to action.

So I ask you. What do you love? Do others know it? Can we see it clearly from your actions or are you wanting others to guess? If you love it, show it.

Prayer: Father God we thank you for your love toward us. You have loved us more than anyone will ever love us. You proved your love on Calvary through your son Jesus Christ. Help us to share the love that you have for us to others in all that we say and do. In Jesus' name we pray. Amen.

God is in the midst of her; she shall not be moved: God shall help her, and that right early. Psalms 46:5

Make The Adjustment

I am a sports fanatic primarily because I have never played team sports. I love to watch other people play and win. I watched every game and even recorded the 2015 NBA Finals. I was torn because I really wanted Lebron James to win for Cleveland but, they just didn't have enough to do it. He is the best basketball player on the planet but, basketball is still a team sport. One man can't do it all. All of the time outs, half time adjustments, pep talks and exchange of players didn't cause them to win.

What adjustments do you need to make in your line up or your strategy to move toward your purpose goals? Whatever that adjustment is, Psalms 46 tells us that God is smack dab right in the middle of it all. He has not gone anywhere. He is on your side. HYou shall not be destroyed. You shall live that abundant life that He promised. Don't give up. God is your help and that Help is Coming Early. He's coming on time and He won't be late.

We have the right God on our side and remember that our God wins every time. No matter what it looks like. He is enough help all by himself. He don't need nobody. He uses us and works through us but, He don't need us.

Whatever you are going through, make the adjustment and know that God is going to give us the victory! Amen!

Prayer: God I thank you that you have won the eternal victory over death and sin. Lord, I ask that you strengthen and strategize me for every battle in my life. In Jesus' name I pray. Amen.

And they beckoned unto their partners, which were in the other ship, that they should come and help them. And they came, and filled both the ships, so that they began to sink.
Luke 5:7 (KJV)

Partners for a Purpose

When my mother was about to cook something new for dinner, she would take the recipe to the store with her. All of the ingredients would be listed and she could just buy everything that was on the recipe. She didn't have to worry whether it was in the kitchen cabinet already. She would buy everything she needed at one time. At home, she would take everything out of the bag and prepare the dish. Simple. No problems and the dinner was great.

But, there are some projects that are not as simple as an entrée for dinner. Some projects take a team to complete. What if you had been working on a project for months? When it is time to complete the project, you have a disagreement or just an emergency arises and the people you counted on to help you suddenly can't? What do you do? You first, pray. You second, pray some more. Then next you look around you for people who are willing to help you.

In the Bible, Peter was an expert fisherman. Jesus told him to launch out into the deep for fish. He did as Jesus told him. Peter caught so many fish that it was about to sink his boat. So Peter called for his partners with their boats to come help him bring the load in. God knew you would have a harvest to bring in. He also knew exactly the people that HE wanted to help you bring it in. My prayer today is that God brings people into your life but, that you recognize them for who they are, "Your Partners for a Purpose."

Prayer: God bless my friends with what they need, who they need and when they need it to fulfill your purpose today!

And the man bowed down his head, and worshipped the Lord. Genesis 24:26

To him that overcometh will I grant to sit with me in my throne, even as I also overcame, and am set down with my Father in his throne. Revelation 3:21

Power Down to Power Up

The word down has such a negative connotation associated with it. There is the economy has taken a down turn, downsizing in corporate America and the morals of this country are going to or have fallen down. But, recently, I have had some down time and realize that the word down should not always be considered negative.

Slow Down so you don't miss something. Going too fast can cause a person to overlook details, forget directions and miss destinations.

I have a job where I walk but, there are times that I can **sit down**, rest my feet and relax. Sitting down is a wonderful feeling if you have been walking, standing, jogging or working at a fast pace. Sitting down also has a posture for your body. The most important is your face, head and eyes are facing forward. When you are sitting down, you can see the forward direction. To me it means, progress, next steps and advancement. So sitting down can't be all bad.

Now, one of my favorites is I don't lie down a lot but, when I do, I am on my back and looking up. I prop myself on my favorite pillows, watch TV, look at the ceiling and pray to my heavenly father. Even though I am lying down, I see up. The progression of moving from down to up. So lying down can't be all bad because when I am finished sleeping, napping or relaxing, watch out, I am getting back up refreshed and ready to do battle.

Finally, one that most people fear and that is **powering down**. To restart or reboot your computer, you should shut it down or power it down and restart it so that it can work properly. The same is with your body and your spirit, not God's Spirit. Power yourself down. As John the Baptist said, "I decrease so that He might increase." You power down and decrease so that you can be powered up or increased by God's Holy Spirit.

When you have a season of sitting down, lying down and powering down, God will allow you to power up with a focused purpose, vision and future.

Prayer: Father I thank you that you have allowed me to slow down, sit down, lie down and power down in your presence. You restored my soul, mind and body. Help me to rise up in your power to do your will and fulfill your purpose. In Jesus' name I pray. Amen.

And it came to pass after this, that Joash was minded to repair the house of the Lord. 2 Chronicles 24:2

For the mountains shall depart, and the hills be removed; but my kindness shall not depart from thee, neither shall the covenant of my peace be removed, saith the Lord that hath mercy on thee. Isaiah 54:10

Repair, Remove, Replace

One of the many things that I love about my husband is that he doesn't like anything in the house that is in need of repair. On the other hand, he doesn't like to replace or purchase things easily. He will go through extensive research, comparison shopping, asking his family and friends before he will spend the money for a purchase. Once he is sure that it can't be repaired by a new part, repairman, screw driver or hammer, he'll purchase a new one.

We don't own a junk or repair service, so we must remove it. There is no sense keeping things in our house that don't work. We get rid of it.

Finally, we purchase something new and hopefully, we research the different manufacturers and look at reviews to buy something even better and will last longer than the previous item.

That principle is true in multiple areas of your life. Make the decision to Repair, Remove or Replace things that are broken in your life. There is no sense hanging around and keeping a person, issue or lifestyle that is broken, repair it. If it cannot be fixed, remove it. After the old is removed, replace it with new habits, thoughts, words, people and places. Life is too short to remain miserable, abused and unhappy. Repair, Remove or Replace today!

Prayer: Father I thank you for power to decide. You have made me a free moral agent. Help me to see the things in my life that are broken. Show me how to repair, remove and/or replace them in my life. Lead and guide me. In Jesus' name I pray. Amen.

But my God shall supply all your need according to his riches in glory by Christ Jesus. Philippians 4:19

Season of Need

In each phase of your life, you have different needs. At one time in my life, I needed to get out of debt. I met a financial advisor and he told me exactly what to do to get out of debt. Fortunately, I did what he said and in a short period of time, I had succeeded. After I met the banker and received the instruction he was relocated from the job and our city. I never saw him again. He was placed in my life to help through that season of need. I know that you have heard the saying, 'people are put in your life for a reason, season or a lifetime.' People may not be meant to stay in your life forever. God might have provided them to answer a question, supply a need or solve a problem in your life. You and that person may move on to something else or another location. It doesn't mean that you don't care, like or love that person any more. It is just that it is over. There will be seasons of need, seasons of abundance, seasons of sorry and seasons of joy. Be grateful for the people who are in your life during every season. Thank God that He brought them but, don't harbor any ill will if they leave. The season of need for that person, place or thing is over.

What do you need at this time in your life? Ask God. He will supply it. After He supplies it, thank Him and thank the person who brought it. Move forward.

Prayer: God I thank you that you have been and will be a supplier of my every need. Guide me through this season in my life and help me to see the good in every situation whether pleasant or unpleasant. In Jesus' name I pray. Amen.

And the Lord smelled a sweet savour; Genesis 8:21

He saith among the trumpets, Ha, ha; and he smelleth the battle afar off, Job 39:25

They have ears, but they hear not: noses have they, but they smell not: Psalm 115:6

Smell of Victory

Thanksgiving is the biggest eating day of all. I don't care if you are eating bologna, chittlins, turkey, Ham, Filet Mignon or cream of wheat just eat it with people you love. The beauty of this day are the smells that come from the kitchen. Oh how sweet and savory are the smells. The smell of collard greens mixed with dressing mixed with turkey mixed with the yeast of rolls mixed with the yams and sweet potato pie make for a wonderful aroma coming from a good southern the kitchen. So, what is the smell that is coming from your life's kitchen? What are you cooking in your life? Are you cooking up love, peace, joy, contentment, creativity and hope or are you giving off the ugly smell of defeat, hatefulness, jealousy, discontent and anger? Right along with the wonderful smells of well-seasoned and cooked food on Thursday will be the garbage in the garbage can or the bacteria in the garbage disposal. On Thursday, when the garbage can gets full, we will take it out quickly. My husband tells me that I am obsessed with getting rid of garbage. There is no need for the ugly smells to mingle with the good smells. It ruins everything. In my life, I strive to do that too, get rid of the garbage quickly. It stinks. It smells bad. It reminds us that something is rottening, dying or defeated around us. It reminds me of Mary speaking to Jesus in John 11:39. Mary responded to Jesus re: Lazarus in the grave, "by now he stinketh." Anything in your life's kitchen stinking? On the other hand, I want God to smell a sweet fragrance coming from the life that He gave me. I want Him to hang out in the kitchen of my life because it smells good in there. I want Him to pull up a chair, loosen His belt, take His shoes off and grab the remote to stay a while and commune with me. I don't want Him to leave early because it doesn't even smell appetizing or desirable. I have battles to fight so I need Him to give me a battle plan, strategy or power to be victorious. I need the smell of victory in, through and all around me. I want people to pass by, look in and take a big whiff of the kitchen of my life and say, I smell victory.

Prayer: Father, be pleased with my offering of praise. Let it be a sweet smelling savor in your nostrils. Give us the sweet smell of victory. In Jesus' name. Amen.

The LORD alone led him; no foreign god was with him.
Deuteronomy 32:12

Standing Alone

The movie "Secretariat" stars Diane Lane based on the true story of Penny Chenery Tweedy, a woman struggling to save her family's horse farm. She obtained a horse and named him "Secretariat." She believed Secretariat could win the triple crown of racing. It had not been done in 25 years but, she believed so much that she faced opposition from the entire racing industry in her quest. She was willing to stand alone in spite of her husband, her brother or investors not believing in her quest.

Her husband could have helped her but, he refused to use his personal money in the effort. Her brother tried to sue her but, came to his senses at the last leg of the Triple Crown when it seemed a great possibility of victory. Her father passed away and she was left with only her employees who were paid to support her.

Have you ever believed in something that you were willing to stand alone to do it, have it or achieve it? You faced opposition, couldn't find anyone to help or who believed in your vision but, continued anyway? Are you willing to stand alone? Do you need the majority rule or support before you move forward? There will be an idea, vision, mission or product that may come along and only you will believe it can happen. What do you do then? Do you go for it or watch it die because of lack of support, help and agreement? Standing alone is not a sign of failure but, should be fuel to fan the flame of victory. Don't get discouraged or quit on what you believe. Be willing to stand alone. In the end Secretariat won the race but, the real victory was the breeding profits that made Secretariat a racing champion and Ms. Tweedy a multi-millionaire many times over. God promised He would bring us into a wealthy place. Are you willing to stand alone?

Prayer: Lord give us that strength to be willing to stand alone in spite of people. Lord, remind us that with you, we are never alone. If you be for us, who can be against us? In Jesus' name we pray. Amen.

God is my strength and power: and he maketh my way perfect. 2 Samuel 22:33

The God Effect

Oprah Winfrey is a media mogul that has made history in this country with her talk shows spotlighting people, books, music, companies and products. Her "Oprah's favorite things" has made companies move from merely making production to multi-million dollar companies seemingly overnight. This is called the "Oprah Effect." If Oprah can do this with her finite power, what about the "God Effect." God has all power, all knowledge and can be everywhere at the same time. There are unlimited possibilities to what God will do and not what He can do. He can do anything. The "God Effect" is favor on steroids. My challenge to you is to stay with, serve and submit to God. There is no telling where He will take you and work in your life. What will you turn over to Him and watch the "God Effect" take effect?

Prayer: God we thank you that with you all things are possible. We rest in your power, strength, wisdom and knowledge. Make our way perfect. In Jesus' name I pray. Amen.

For by grace are ye saved through faith; and that not of yourselves: it is the gift of God: Not of works, lest any man should boast. Ephesians 2:8-9

But Noah found grace (favor) in the eyes of the Lord. Genesis 6:8

The Grace with My Gift

There have been dreams, desires, visions and goals that I have had in my life. These dreams, desires, visions and goals were not necessarily bad or sinful but, they were not in God's will for my life. He didn't give me the grace for this project, assignment or endeavor. As much as He has gifted, assigned and anointed me to do, there are some things in my life that God has said no. I didn't have the grace for it. I had the skill. I could have learned any new skill required but, God said no. He didn't put His stamp of approval or favor on me to do a certain thing, position or be a certain place in life. On the other hand, there are things that God has called me specifically to do, places to be and people to minister to. At times, it is uncomfortable, it goes against my personal grain and I pray hard to do it. In the end, I always know, God gave me His grace or favor or stamp of approval to do it. Even when it does turn out like I want it to and the recognition or appreciation for what was done is not there, He says, "I am pleased and that is all that matters." As I am getting older, looking myself hard in the mirror and being real with who I am; I thank God for His Grace on my life. In this stage of my life, I realize that it is time out for being fake, phony or pretending. It is time to get down to 'the core' of who you are and what you were called to be. At the core, you will realize what you are supposed to be doing and the Grace of God will be on your purpose, passion and define project. In all that you do, don't forget to thank God for "The Grace for It."

Prayer: God I thank you that you have granted me Grace with my Gift. I don't deserve any Grace on my Gift but, I seek to live my life and use my Gift to give you glory and honor for the Grace you have given to me. In Jesus' name I pray. Amen.

Trust in the Lord with all thine heart; and lean not unto thine own understanding. In all thy ways acknowledge him, and he shall direct thy paths. Proverbs 3:5-6

The Trust Factor

There is a team building exercise that requires each person to be blind folded and walk in a straight line. The only exception is that the person in front is not blindfolded. The person in the front not blind folded is designated the leader. The leader speaks clear, precise step by step directions to move the entire group from one location to the next and then to the final destination. Some team building exercises may involve climbing stairs, passing through doorways and other obstacle courses. You cannot see your way. You can only listen your way. You can only go by the directions you hear given by the person who can see.

In this exercise, trust now has a capital T. You have to trust the leader and trust each other to tell you how many steps, when to stop and when to start to get to the final destination. It takes time, it's scary but, if successful, it can be a rewarding experience. This exercise is designed for each member of the team to come away with a greater trust in each other built through the exercise. The ultimate goal is that this trust that is built will be transferred to every endeavor, activity, product or service that this team desires to initiate.

We cannot see God but, we can hear His voice speaking to us all the time. He speaks either audibly, directly or indirectly through other people and circumstances. Staying close to God we can follow His directions and reach our destination. The spiritual trust factor involves our faith and hope that we will reach our final destination only through hearing the voice of God. We have faith in God because He is God. We have trust in God based on all that He is done from history until now. Our faith and trust causes us to hope for the brighter, abundant life that He promised and will deliver.

Look at your circumstances and realize, God has the power, plan and purpose but, it is our duty to initiate the Trust Factor in God to bring every situation to a victorious conclusion.

Prayer: Father, I thank you that you have always made ways, provided answers and been there with me through every circumstance. In the words of the hymn, "oh for Grace to trust you more." In Jesus Name I Pray. Amen.

For God so loved the world, that he gave his only begotten Son, that whosoever believeth in him should not perish, but have everlasting life." John 3:16 (KJV)

The Power of One

There is an old song with the lyrics, "one is the loneliest number that you'll ever do." That may be true in love or trying to work out but, one is powerful. Jesus prayed to the father, Lord make them one as you and I are one." There was also a tower about to be built to heaven if God hadn't confused their language because the people were one. Unity is wonderful and we can get more done if we act, work and believe as one. But, have you ever had one idea, thought, person or opportunity change your whole life? I heard a message from Bishop Jakes one time and still don't remember the title, but I resigned from my church, resigned a national position and set out on a journey that I knew not but, only had one word. One word led me to a new church, new job, new businesses, new city/state, new husband and new life. We all know that one vote can make the difference between winning and losing an election but, one word, one hug and one encouragement can save a marriage, business or life. Don't let your one be seen as small because one man, Jesus changed the entire world because He was willing to say that one yes and make the ultimate sacrifice just one time. Will you be that one? Have a great day.

Prayer: Father, I thank you that you sent your one and only son to redeem a world. Use me to be a person who blesses someone today and always. In Jesus' name I pray. Amen.

The word of the LORD came to me: "What do you see...
Jeremiah 1:11 (NIV)

What do you see?

The ability to see is very important to me. I thank God every day for the ability to see. I have worn glasses since I was eight years old. I couldn't see the chalk board in third grade and began getting poor grades. The grades were poor because I was sitting in the back of the class writing down the wrong numbers in math and the wrong words in spelling and subsequently getting the wrong answer. The teacher suggested to my parents that I see an eye doctor. I have been wearing glasses or contact lenses ever since. The ability to see correctly was the key to academic success. The teacher used the blackboard for teaching everything and your job was to copy it down from the board. At the end of the day, the boards were all erased and cleaned for the next day. So seeing was critical to learning. In the spirit world, the ability to see spiritually is even more important than seeing physically. There are those who can see with their natural eyes but, don't have a clue spiritually what is going on around them. Elisha said on one occasion "open <u>thou</u> the young man's eyes." What do you see? I realize that we can all be in the same place, seeing the same show or service and still see differently. It all depends on our focus and emphasis. What do you see? Seeing is critical to movement. If you are unsure of what lies ahead, you move more slowly and cautiously until you can get clear vision. What do you see? Some people move more slowly because of what they do see. The path ahead may be difficult or unpleasant so one may become hesitant and slow their steps. So what do you see? Admit it when you are driving on a clear day, you drive much faster and arrive to your destination much quicker. It is the same in the spiritual world. When you see where God wants to take you, you should move toward it, obey the commands and go through the process much faster and quicker to arrive at your destination.

See with your natural eyes and your spiritual eyes. What do you see for your family, career, business, church or ministry? Put no confidence in what you see now because it is temporary. Ask God for His eyes to see what He sees for your present, purpose and destiny. Finally, remember no matter how bad it looks to you, God sees the same thing. He knows exactly where you are, what you are doing and what you are seeing.

Prayer: God you have perfect eyes into my life. Let me see how you see. Help me to trust you more in spite of what I do see with my natural eyes. In Jesus' name I pray. Amen.

A good man out of the good treasure of his heart bringeth forth that which is good; and an evil man out of the evil treasure of his heart bringeth forth that which is evil: for of the abundance of the heart his mouth speaketh. Luke 6:45

What's in your mouth?

Now you might look at the title of this article and say that sounds like the credit card commercial, "What's in your wallet?" The credit card is designed to buy things that you are not yet able to pay for or to bring into possession things that you will pay for later. The words may seem similar but, the message is a little different. Your words have so much power they are creating things and bringing things into your possession whether you have money or not. Today, remind yourself to be careful about what is coming out of your mouth. The words coming out of your mouth stem from the thoughts going on in your head. You have a choice whether to speak them or not. God taught us the power of words when He created the heaven, earth and everything in it. Watch out what you say. Not only do you hear your words, God hears your words and so too does the enemy. The enemy can bring opportunities and situations to you that can create negative situations. God controls everything and can cause good to come out of a bad situation but, don't help the enemy! So what's in your mouth? The power of life and death is in your tongue which is located in your mouth. A gun is not the only thing that can kill. Saying the wrong thing with your mouth and it will take tear down, destroy and demolish the situation just as nicely as an AK-47. What is your mouth? Speak health, prosperity and the abundant life today.

Prayer: Father, I thank you for the ability to praise and thank you with my mouth. Let the words of my mouth be pleasing to you now and always. In Jesus' name I pray. Amen.

www.ingramcontent.com/pod-product-compliance
Lightning Source LLC
Chambersburg PA
CBHW050648160426
43194CB00010B/1851